Kingdom Publishers

A Curious Collection of Christian Poems

Copyright © Joanna Yusuf

All rights reserved. No part of this book may be reproduced in any form by photocopying or any electronic or mechanical means, including information storage or retrieval systems, without permission in writing from both the copyright owner and the publisher of the book. The right of Joanna Yusuf to be identified as the author of this work has been asserted by her in accordance with the Copyright, Designs and Patents Act 1988 and any subsequent amendments thereto.
A catalogue record for this book is available from the British Library.

All Scripture Quotations have been taken from the New International Version and the King James Version of the Bible.

ISBN: 978-1-913247-62-1

1st Edition by Kingdom Publishers
Kingdom Publishers
London, UK.

You can purchase copies of this book from any leading bookstore or email
contact@kingdompublishers.co.uk

DEDICATION

Joanna would first like to dedicate this book to our God Almighty, who has been her constant source of comfort and inspiration throughout the years. She would also like to thank the following people for their immense help in the preparation of the book. Her dear Sister Sunbo, who has not only always been supportive of her passion for poetry, but has also given up her time and energy to assist in the preparation of this book, and Paul and Hermione Puzey, (Pastors of Redhill Christian Fellowship) whose assistance has been invaluable in this process.

CONTENTS

What God is to Mankind

To the Historian, He is the beginning

He created the world and everything in it

To those in darkness, He is the light

That light that sparkles so very bright.

To the needy, He's Jehovah Jireh

This just means He's our provider

To the potter, He is his maker

And He's bread of life to the baker.

To the journalist, He is good news

News filled with holy views

To the soldier, He is some warrior

And to the unsaved, what a Saviour!

To the scholar, He is the word

Which is sharper than any two-edged sword

He is the physician to the doctor

While to the accused, an advocator.

To the astronaut, He's the morning star

Easily detected on your spiritual radar

He's the spring of living water to the thirsty

This water refreshes both spirit and body.

To the lost, He is the way

But what a price He had to pay

He's the lily of the valley to the gardener

While to the carpenter, hey! He was a carpenter.

To the troubled, He's the Prince of Peace

So only He, can troubles cease

To the present generation, He is I AM

But also, too, the sacrificial lamb.

To the child, He's Abba Father
And yet to the servant, He's the master
He is a friend to the confessed sinner
And turns them into a spiritual winner.

To all royalty, He is the King of Kings
It is good to bow down and worship Him
And finally, He is God to everyone
We have everlasting life, through His Son.

Being Alone
with God

If in God's kingdom, you hope to bear fruit

Or if you spiritually hope to thrive

If you desire to undertake gigantic exploits

And have the Lord Jesus as your guide

If you hope to blitz your problems

And remain faithful despite the odds

Jesus is saying, "you need to practice the art

of being alone with God".

It is the prayer of faith that brings blessings

To the people that we meet

It is the prayer of hope that brings about

The specific answers that we seek

To those persisting problems

That refuse to go away

Jesus is saying, "to be victorious

We need to go to God and pray".

The devil is busy deceiving people

And doing exactly what he pleases

By afflicting anyone and everyone

With sicknesses and diseases

The only way to subdue him

Is not to retire to the land of nod

But rather, it's to go to your closet

And practice the art of being alone with God.

Some Types
of Christians

Agreed, 'a Wheelbarrow Christian' is quite sincere

He's probably born again, and often a dear

His mates, co-workers, and Christian brethren

All know he never misses a sermon.

He may go to church week after week

Always read his bible at Jesus' feet

He can move mountains, during prayer times he loves

But just like a wheelbarrow, only when shoved.

A 'Borderline Christian', as his name implies

Pitches his tent at the borderline

He's not keen on commitment, and at short notice takes off

But as they say, a rolling stone gathers no moss.

You see, staying right there is too close to the edge

Work out your Salvation Jesus said

While he loves the part where he gets to receive

He's not so keen, to trust and believe.

A 'Busy Lizzie Christian' is rushed off her feet

She works so hard, I'm not sure she sleeps

For the Lord? I hear you ask, I wouldn't like to say

She's been so busy that she's found no time to pray.

Miss Biss starts her day with her breakfast of toast

Following that she's running around, from pillar to post

After sharing the word with the lost, she's back on the road

When God wants a word, she puts him on hold.

'Point the Finger Christian', thinks he's always right

And to defend his corner, he's prepared to argue and fight

Albeit, he reads his bible and oversees the church keys

He still needs to learn the art of 'agreeing to disagree'.

Last week, during the team meeting, 'Point the Finger' saw red

After he took exception at something, someone else said

He promptly said his piece, gathered his stuff and refused to linger

After which, the meeting crashed, all because of 'Point the Finger'.

Now a Mature Christian is not perfect you know

But with God, he doesn't resist but goes with the flow

He carries his cross, up that tough narrow road

And presents himself, as a vessel of gold.

He strives to go up, onto higher ground

And share the precious gifts he's found

But when God looks down from heaven above

How He looks on all the different Christians, with such mercy and love.

1. Some Types of Christians

That Big Old Comfy Chair

My heart is my dear Lord's dwelling place

Which is where we'd regularly meet

Yahweh seated, in a big, old comfy armchair

And me sitting beside Him, in my own little modest seat.

Our appointment times have been set and locked

At the start of every day

And boy, am I so thankful for this

Otherwise, things would keep going astray.

During these times, I would listen carefully

To everything my Lord would say

And I would home-in on His advanced wisdom and knowledge

And meditate on it, night and day.

Yahweh has so many wonderful sides

He's our Father, our Maker, our Boss

He also loves us all so very much

He allowed His son die for us on the cross.

But still I started to get very distracted

As my life legged it to a difficult place

Leaving me feeling harassed and exhausted

And sadly, we'd no longer meet face to face.

As time went by, I returned to the scene of my heart

And by the window, I did take a quick peep

I was both surprised and bewildered to see my Lord

Still seated in that big, old comfy seat.

I then knew instinctively that I had to pop in

And at least throw up a rather self-conscious 'hi'

I also needed to know, and so awkwardly asked

Why, despite my absence, He had still chosen to drop by.

He replied, "my child, I have seen your pain

But sadly noticed, faith was exchanged for despair

But I knew you would eventually remember my Word

So, I chose to come daily and wait in that spot we both share".

Tears filled my eyes as I ran to my Lord

And apologized for not kneeling in prayer

I'm so grateful, He did not simply just go on his way

But chose to wait in that big, old comfy chair.

2. That Big Old Comfy Chair

Trying Times!

When frustration and problems are all around

And peace and serenity cannot be found

When you want to laugh, but can only cry

When you yearn to live, but also want to die

When Satan sends threats that are menacing, but clear

Rest if you must, but please persevere.

When life is unstable, and your path is not straight

When the questions you ask are met with answers you hate

When that cloak of darkness leaves you unable to see

When you're tied up in knots, but you want to be free

When you're pushed and squeezed, and so you're always subdued

Hold on, you might be nearing that long awaited-breakthrough.

When your income is low, but your outgoings are high

And you have to be careful with everything that you buy

 When you want to socialize, but you're told to stay home

Instead of celebrating with friends, you end up celebrating alone

When absolutely everything seems in complete disarray

It possibly means 'victory' is heading your way.

When 'failure' seems 'bold', and 'progress' seems 'shy'

And when loss outshines profit, and you can't understand why

When all your hard work seems to reap very little reward

And it appears the rules of fair-play are simply being ignored

When you feel life has thrown you its toughest blow yet

 You need to bounce back to your feet, rather than stay down and
fret.

Friends, please make no mistake, God is always in control

And so nothing ever happens, without first, His say so

His perfect plan for your life will surely come to pass

If you place your trust in Him, and then, stay steadfast

So when things are chaotic, and you're at loss what to do

It's time to reach out to our Father in heaven, and He will sure
pull you through.

3. Trying Times

Pure Truths

"For God so loved the world that he gave his only begotten son, that whosoever believes in Him should not perish but have everlasting life" (John 3:16)

That's what God did

"The fear of the Lord is the beginning of knowledge" (Proverbs 1:7)

That's from God's Word

"I have come that they may have life, and that they may have it more abundantly" (John 10:10b)

Jesus said that

"Let the words of my mouth and the meditation of my heart be acceptable in your sight, O Lord, my strength and my redeemer" (Psalms 19:14)

That is my prayer

"Do not sorrow, for the joy of the Lord is my strength" (Nehemiah 8:10b)

I say Amen

"Let your light so shine before men, that they may see your good works and glorify your Father in heaven" (Matthew 5:16)

Help me O Lord

"I can do all things through Christ, who strengthens me" (Philippians 4:13)

He is our source

"Greater is He that is in me, than he that is in the world" (1 John 4:4b)

That is my truth

You are my loving Father

That's who You are

I am lavishly loved by You

That's who I am.

Bible Quotes from the new Kings Version

Is It The Best?

There's nothing wrong with making the number one person you

Except on the last day, you may be at the back of the queue

There's nothing wrong with doing just enough to get by

But you'll have nothing extra to show God when you die.

There's nothing wrong with running from the problems you face

Except, you'll be running a frustrating race

There's nothing wrong with keeping the good news to yourself

But you won't be keeping any heavenly wealth.

There's nothing wrong closing, to your neighbour, your door

Except, spiritually, you may remain poor

There's nothing wrong with fighting, not forgiving your foe

But when you, yourself sin, will forgiveness flow?

There's nothing wrong with keeping everything that you own

But you then don't sow seeds, so crops will not grow

There's nothing wrong having your own way, I guess

Absolutely nothing wrong, but is it the best?

4. Is It The Best?

Jesus and
His Business Card

(If Jesus had a business card, I would surmise it would record the following information)

Company Name: Life Changer

Contact Name: Jesus Christ

Address of Company: The Body of Christ, Church Road, World

Email: Prayer@God.com

Where you can find us: In the Holy Bible

The Life changer is a family business that has been in operation for 2000 years since Jesus moved His location (traveling millions of miles from Heaven to Earth).

This company comprises of Management, which is the Godhead (i.e. God the Father, God the Son, and God the Holy Spirit). They in turn employ a large number of Heavenly Hosts.

Some of the qualities they display include; holy and righteous living, loving-kindness, compassion, wisdom, knowledge, understanding, and forgiveness. They have a sound reputation for being available for their clients over and beyond all expectations. In fact, their track record regarding their area of expertise is literally out of this world. They receive great reviews from all their customers/clients, who continually sing their praises, and unreservedly testify to their goodness at every opportune moment.

The company covers all aspects of salvation, forgiveness, deliverance, and healing, to name but a few of its many services. These services can help/support individuals, communities, countries, and in fact the whole entire world. Please note that this company also incorporates "deep cleansing facilities" which can eradicate the worst stains, which come from heavy-duty sin.

The Company or Business is open 24/7, and the good news is that there is only Good News!.

Further perks of the Company are as follows:

Clients will be treated like royalty (children of the King).

All messages left via prayer will be fast-tracked to the Managing Director (or should I say our Heavenly Father), and He will respond, with the right answer, at the right time.

The Company/Clientele Contact Model (CCCM) will operate under an 'up close and personal basis', with the owner of the Company, Yahweh Himself, being accessible via his Son Jesus Christ. Wow! this is big, people.

You might also like to know, that once you sign into this business, and agree to the terms and conditions, (i.e. accepting that we are sinners and that only Jesus can save/set us free and reunite us with His Father), you will automatically be insured against evil entities, including the spirit of fear, the spirit of deception, the spirit of temptation, and all the other nasties that hangout in the kingdom of darkness.

Did I mention that this company is a non-profit organization? which means everything on offer in terms of gifts, services, utilities, & blessings, etc. are all free of charge, and will not cost you an arm or a leg. However, that said, it did actually cost the Company owner, (or our Heavenly Father), a bit more than that, it did in fact cost Him His only begotten Son, for our sakes.

And yes, I do see the incredulity on your face, and absolutely get it.

I hear you quoting; "If it's too good to be true, it is probably just that, too good to be true".

Well to the "quoters", the response from this company is as follows:

"God is good, and His Son is true

That man-made quote? That is not God's view

Because He drew up a new contract that is lasting and new

And it holds the blueprint for our great rescue

So, all you who are lost and don't have a clue

The good news is that Jesus laid down His life for you

And while this is the best news ever, it's also 100% true

Remember friends, this business is God's business. It is an absolute Life Changer.

It is a Must for everyone who wants to invest in their eternity and ensure that when they retire from this life, they will be with Jesus, our Saviour, and our Heavenly Father who loves all of us dearly.

No other business can ever come close to guaranteeing such wonderful and significant promises.

Please, don't just take my word for it only, take God's word from:

John 3:16 - *For God so loved the World, that He gave His only begotten Son so that whoever believes in Him, shall not perish, but have everlasting life.*

Luke 3:49 - *Why is it that you sought me, did you not know, I must be about my Father's business.*

John 14:6 - *I am the way, the truth, and the life, no one comes to the Father except through me.*

Amen/ Emuna (Emuna in Hebrew means - I believe)

Thank You

Scripture quote - New King James version

5. Jesus and His Business Card

The Mentally Ill

It's good to visit the hospitals and support the very sick

When you see patients in agony, you pray for healing real quick

But what about the chap who's violent? And may even try to kill

He also needs our prayers, because you see, he's mentally ill.

He may not be the normal patient who stays quietly in his bed

He may give you a really hard time because of what's going on in his head

When you speak, he may not listen or even understand

But still, he desperately needs our prayers, so let's give him a prayerful hand.

It's good to visit the prisons, because you are blessed, and in turn can bless

It's exciting when the inmates turn to Christ, but we still can't afford to rest

Because there are some segregated, they're known as a different kind

They need prayers because they are imprisoned twice, physically and in their mind.

And what about the homeless? those sleeping rough on the streets

Having no money to buy food and going days with nothing to eat

It is said 'help' is around, that at last, they have been given a choice

But the mentally ill among them may neither be heard nor have a voice.

It's quite understandable that many fall by the way

And it's sad that they are totally misunderstood, by our society of today

They can't stay in the hospital forever, and in jail will they receive the best care?

They need God, but who will take them to church, they need love, but for them that is rare.

Jesus really loves them and for them His life He gave

So, can it be they will suffer on earth, and still in the end not be saved?

So, for all the folk who are mentally ill, and find it so hard to cope

The next stanza is a message for you, a special message of hope.

You see, nothing is impossible with God, He can help to sow the right seed

In fact, Jesus said "if the Son sets you free, you shall be free indeed

Please God give us knowledge and wisdom, the strength to pray until

We have a deeper understanding and can be there for the mentally ill.

6. The Mentally Ill

Does God Need Rest

The other day, I dabbled with fire and consequently got burnt

I guess it was to be expected, but with pain this lesson I learnt

I ran to my Father in heaven, His face I decided to seek

But He simply said, "my child I am on holiday, I suggest you come back next week".

I played with Mr. Temptation, and in hindsight, this wasn't me at my best

Because I found things turning tricky, and my life became such a mess

Sobbing, I ran to Lord Jesus, who has great restoring and transforming powers

But He simply said, "my dear, I suggest you come back during office hours."

I went on a self-referred journey, it seemed like a good idea at the time

But problems arose from decisions made, and quite simply they were all mine

Again, I went to call on my Lord Jesus, to ask what I should do for the best

He simply said, "today is the Sabbath, as you know, it is my day of rest".

Hands up, I failed to place my Lord at the centre, and as a result, took an undignified fall

But, when sharing my sorrows with Jesus my Lord, He seemed not to respond to my call

Ashamed of my thoughts, I return to my Saviour, to simply plead my case with Him

But now I'm getting extremely concerned when He said "my dear, I'm just about to turn in."

Although I'm confused and troubled, I must get the attention of my Redeemer and Friend

I read what He says in the Bible, about being with me to the end

"So, what has gone so wrong Lord, for it's you I desperately seek"

My heavenly Father said, "I'm right here my child, but you have been fast asleep".

My Conversation at the Doctors

Here I am at the doctor's again, waiting you see

And, as usual, the place was as packed as can be

I sighed heavily as I quickly said a silent prayer

When I looked up again, I saw a man seated near.

Staring intensely at my badge, he asked, "what does that mean?"

"It simply means I'm born again", I replied getting very keen

He said, "fancy being born twice, is not once enough for man?"

"To me, it beats dying twice, I much prefer this plan."

He had a little think, and asked, "you think Jesus is our King?"

Yes, I confirmed, "but not only that, I know He lives within"

He said, "I find that hard to buy, cos they say seeing is believing"

"Well," I said, "I have since learned that believing is simply seeing."

He talked about this life, how he strived to make it in the past

But I said, "unlike with God, things in this world don't last"

He said to me, "to reach the top, it helps to be of noble birth"

I replied, "that to reach the top, our King had to serve."

We then changed topics and started talking about food

He, thinking it a safer topic, settled into a lighter mood

He said, "it follows, the more you eat, the less you need to stuff your face"

I replied, "but the more you eat the word of God, the more you want to taste."

"OK," he said, "the more you give, the less you have, don't tell me that it pays"

"The more you give, the more you have in so many better ways"

That's when he asked, "To be God's child, what must I do?"

I gladly replied, "confess your sins, and believe He died for you."

"Mr. Hope, your next," said a nurse entering the room

I hadn't noticed, the room was now empty, and my watch showed it was noon

Who says God does not hear, and God does not answer prayer

You see, when I first arrived here, I prayed, please make my time here rich and rare.

7. My Conversation at the Doctors

What Am I

I know I am important, that's a major clue

Crying out to the living God is something I can do *(Psalm 84:2)*

I work 24/7 and have no time to play

In fact, I will only retire, on my dying day.

Wherever your treasures are, that's where I am also *(Matthew 6:21)*

But having said that, I'm not only there - I'm everywhere you go

Rivers of living water can flow right out of me *(John 7:38)*

It's a tremendous giveaway, puzzled? You shouldn't be.

Another good tip is the fact I can actually instruct you   *(Psalm 16:7)*

I can also rejoice in the Lord, that's another great thing
I can do

Apart from our heavenly Father, no one can normally   *(1 Samuel 16:7)*
see me

Apart from our heavenly Father, no one can stay
within me.

I don't think I've mentioned, er, my other darker side

I can become real evil, when Satan becomes the guide

Yes, Satan can fill me up and take me further and   *(Acts 5:3)*
further

Down the slippery evil path, which can lead to death   *(Matthew 15:19)*
and murder.

Yet another interesting thing about me is that I can be   *(Ezekial 11:19)*
stone or flesh

I can also be very pure, and that is me at my very best   *(Matthew 5:8)*

The cool thing about this is the fact God I can actually
see

But on the other hand sadly, things can still trouble me.   *(John 14:1)*

On the odd occasion, I have been known to be real   *(Proverbs 21:4)*
proud

But, ironically, pride is not something that I enjoy
boasting about out loud

I'd rather talk about my work, and as it happens, it
is another crucial clue

Because if my work ceases, unfortunately so do
you.

Well my friend, with all these clues, do you know
who or what I am?

I guess you've established the fact that I'm neither
a woman nor man

Well time has gone, I have to go, but before I will
depart

In case you haven't figured it out, I'm your one and
only heart.

8. What Am I?

Lesson From the Bible

I'm stepping back into history

And will be going on various selective dates

You see, I would like to get a deeper insight

Of our distinguished bible's 'greats'.

I'd like to see how unique they were

And what really made them tick

And perhaps learn something different about them

As I tune into their lives and their challenges.

So, first I will visit king David

Who was renowned for his pursuit of God's own heart

I will then turn my focus to Noah

Who, in the face of mockery, built the Ark.

Next, and as a result of his astonishing faith

God made a lasting covenant with Abraham

And then, I note the pure determination of Ruth

Who left her kinfolk to follow Naomi to Bethlehem.

The impressive anointing of Elijah

Enabled him to accurately prophesy

And of course, the amazing visions that Paul experienced

Which took him into the heavens beyond the sky.

It would be super cool to interpret dreams

And who could do it better than Joseph

And then that long trek to the promised land

Showed longevity and leadership by Moses.

Now, let's look at the physical strength of Samson

Who, even in chains, was still a threat

I would gladly accept the wisdom of Solomon

His intellect amazed just about everyone he met.

Father, let me see the boldness in Daniel

Who refused to compromise his faith

But even when thrown into the lion's den

He always knew Yahweh would keep him safe.

Having returned from my amazing travels

And reflecting on the things I have been privileged to see

My Lord said that in order to join this inclusive club

The following protocol would be the key.

He said that the reason the people I'd seen were so special

And had stayed under His Protection, Mercy, and Grace

Was because they had allocated time to be in His Presence

And had mastered the art of seeking His face.

9. Lesson from the Bible

Blessings in
Today's World

This world we're in, where people sin

There's a huge amount of violence

But on the other side, where such things can't hide

Sin is reduced to silence.

The poor out there, whose cupboards are bare

And stomachs are often empty

One day they'll be as full as can be

In a place where there'll always be plenty.

In these modern times, lots of crimes

Catches the media's attention

But heaven's view is this is not news

And will definitely receive no mention.

If you live alone, or you're on your own

People can sometimes be phony

But there's a region out there where people do care

And you will never ever be lonely.

At work, if you don't belong, and things go wrong

The place can become quite stressful

All people fit in, where Jesus is King

And work stays serene and restful.

To have to spend to keep a friend

I find it quite distasteful

But friendship's stronger, over yonder

Where life is much more graceful.

The kids we know, with an innocent glow

Have been found to be quite cunning

The kids we'll meet, on that golden street

I've been told they are very stunning.

When wives live in fear, of those they hold dear

It really is quite alarming

But up above, with those they love

Their dearest will always stay charming.

As people grow old, they can be left in the cold

And for them, life holds little pleasure

But somewhere in space, in some special place

People stay young and strong forever.

Now! down here below, are a bunch of folk I know

Who are special, I won't keep you guessing

They're people I see every day, could be at work or in a cafe

Who are kind-hearted, and to our world such a blessing.

The Armour of God

Clothes, apparel, attire, call them what you may

They are placed high on our agenda, in our society of today

They include dresses, trousers, jackets, to mention but a few

Some trends are regarded as boring, while others are considered cool.

Clothes cover our bodies and keep us warm and safe

Clothes can give protection and can vary from place to place

But the armed forces wear uniforms, before going out to war

And it will tell all concerned which side they're fighting for.

As a Christian Soldier, the clothes that I must wear

It is the armour of God, which dazzles the enemy, and will never wear or tear

It's an honour to wear this armour, God made it for you and me

It's a valuable gift, and so not cheap, but listen, folks, it's free.

It comprises of my belt, which around my waist I tie

It signifies the truth, as to why Jesus had to die

But praise the Lord, He rose again! When I wear my belt, I see

How for all mankind it was paramount, He died upon that tree.

Then there's my breastplate, full of righteousness

It's the righteousness of Jesus, so guaranteed to be the best

It protects me from those certain darts, the enemy throws at me

But when I claim that righteousness, the enemy has to flee.

See my beautiful shoes, signifying the spread of the gospel of peace

They not only unite nations but help raging wars cease

Whenever you go out walking and meet people on the street

Spread the message behind the shoes you are wearing on your feet.

Another part of my armour is my shield of faith

It will expose the enemy and all his lies, and ensure that I am safe

To keep my shield in prime condition, God's Word I have to hear

For God's Word will help build up my faith, and make my mountains disappear.

My helmet of salvation protects my little head

When the enemy tries to pull me down, Jesus lifts me up instead

My helmet of salvation won for me the victory

My helmet of salvation broke my chains and set me free.

The sword of the Spirit is the weapon that I need

To keep it sharp at all times, the word I have to read

It can do tremendous damage, and hurt the enemy you can tell

Because at the living Word of God Our Father, the enemy has to bow.

Before wearing my armour, and reaching for my goal

My inner garment I must wear, it's plain and rather dull

Jesus himself wore it, and then passed it on to me

Yes, of course, it's that special cloak of humility.

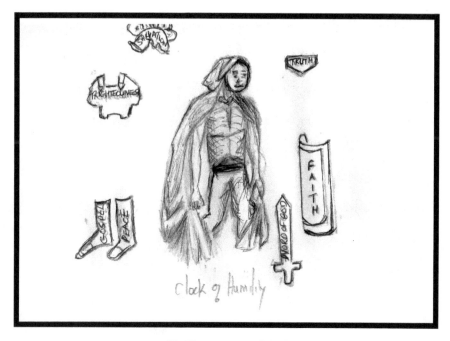

10. The Armour of God

God's Words - A Spiritual Exercise?

The Word of God will enable us to;

"Seek *first the kingdom of God and His righteousness, and all these things shall be added to you"*
- Matthew 6:33

Bow *- "Oh come, let us worship and **_bow_** down; let us kneel before the Lord, our Maker!"*
- Psalm 95:6

*"**_Follow_** me, and I will make you fishers of men"*
- Matthew 4:19

*"**_Walk_** in the Spirit, and you shall not fulfill the lust of the flesh"*
- Galatians 5:16

*"**Resist** the devil and he will flee from you"*
- James 4:7

*** Run** - "Let us **run** with endurance the race that is set before us"*
- Hebrews 12:1

*** Do** -   "I can **do** all things through Christ who strengthens me"*
- Philippians 4:13

*"**Go** therefore and make disciples of all the nations, baptizing them in the name of the Father and of the Son and of the Holy Spirit"*
- Matthew 28:19

*** Fight** - "I have fought the good **fight**, I have finished the race, I have kept the faith"*
- 2 Timothy 4:7

Amen!

Scripture verses from The New King James Version

11. God's Words - A Spiritual Exercise?

Folks On
My Street

Now look at Fred

Must be in pain

Cold hands, sore head

Should really be

At home in bed

But he goes out witnessing, he must be kind

The weather's ghastly, yet he doesn't mind.

Now look at Brad

He is so strange

Always grumpy, looks sad

He's only pleased

When he's done bad

When people see him, they keep away

Only his pet dog, with him, will stay.

What about Stan?

He's apparently rich

But a stingy man

That's what I'm made

To understand

He is quite lonely and doesn't he know

That he's only reaping what he did sow.

Then there's Bill

Who just got married

To his wife Jill

And they were both happy

Till he got ill

Jill is now learning the rest of that verse

Which goes like this, 'for better, for worse'.

Then finally Ray

He must be poor

One room, low pay

Needs special prayers

To survive each day

Yet he helps the homeless, so good is he

I think I'll have him round for tea.

12. Folks on My Street

The Gifts

I think gifts are wonderful, I can see you all agree

They could come in the shape of an outing or even a bigger TV

What a shame, you only receive them at Christmas, or events of that kind

But listen-in, there are some special gifts which you can have any time.

I'll start with the gift of wisdom, that's the wisdom beyond our years

Just like Solomon in the Bible, who was much wiser than his peers

This special wisdom from God will help me when I pray

And in those tricky moments, will guide me on what to say.

Next out comes the gift of Faith, from that massive sack up there

I mean, the faith that moves mountains, which is so very rare

Our Lord exercised this faith when raising Lazarus from the dead

And greater work we will do, that's what our Lord Jesus said.

Now onto the gift of healing, what an honour you understand

When we see people in pain, we can put out a healing hand

Though we have to be sensitive and listen to what God has to say

It would be tricky, messy, and unproductive if we insisted on having our way.

The gift of the working of miracles can be a definite sign

To the lost, poor, and low hearted, and even those who think they're fine

Thousands followed our Lord after the wonders they saw in his day

And how exciting to know now He's gone, He said we should show them the way.

On to the gift of knowledge, such a gift cannot be bought

And when you need such knowledge, it silently comes to thought

How it gives clear insight, to things that baffle you

Also, as part of the package comes instructions on what to do.

Oh, to speak words of comfort, sing songs of exhortation

And also, directly from God, say words of encouragement and edification

Such a really noble gift, whatever can it be?

Yes, of course, it's that glorious gift, the gift of prophesy.

The speaking in different tongues is another gift from our King

It's speaking in a mystery language that no one knows except Him

But He does give interpretations, which if He gave me, I'd do my best

To interpret those different tongues so others can be blessed.

All these gifts are much better, as you can surely see

Then the old routine outing, or even a bigger TV

Would I want the whole bagful though? It would surely wear me down

Because these gifts are not meant for keeping, but to share with a needy town.

God shares them out equally, to his children, like me and you

And when we stand as one body, there's nothing we cannot do

Thank you, Holy Spirit, these gifts will aid us in our strife

And we must not forget to thank our dear Lord, for the gift of eternal life.

13. The Gifts

You Choose!

Is it safer to fear man, who can kill or lies tell?

Or to fear our creator, who can save us from hell

Should you bow to man's voice or the voice of our Lord's?

Though His Word is lasting and sharper, than any two-edged sword.

Would you rather be liked, although you might sin?

Or do right by our Lord and be obedient to Him

Do you prefer earthly presents, which certainly won't last?

Or be blessed with holy gifts, which can help keep you steadfast.

To have a perishable mansion, would that be your dream?

Or to have a home built by Jesus, which will surpass any house that you've seen

Where are you going, you're not sure and don't care?

Or are you making the right choices to reach heaven, and dwell with God there?

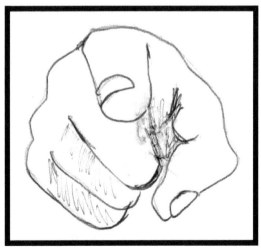

14. You Choose!

Our Final Destination

(My imaginary perception of our final Journey
to Our Father's Kingdom)

Attention to all fellow travelers

Our Father in Heaven is calling all of you out of the wilderness

To a place where your own individual driven-intervention awaits
you.

This tailor-made intervention will convey you to the path, which
will lead you to the truth, which will set you free.

Free to take advantage of a seat aboard the gospel train,
which will transport you straight to 'Free-Will' Train Station. At
Free-Will-Station, you will (coincidentally) exercise your Free
Will to dump your excess baggage of sin, at the Cross.

Please feel free, to shop at our Grace-Free (as opposed to duty-free) stores, where we have on display perfectly designed, snow-white robes of righteousness.

You will be delighted to know that all these garments are grace-free pieces, and so despite their costly price tag, Jesus our Saviour has agreed to step in and foot the entire bill for all of us. This is inclusive of the young, the old, the rich, and the poor. Not only that ladies & gentlemen, I understand that as an additional bonus, you all get to take home a durable & hard-wearing cloak of humility as well.

With your dress code now sorted, you can now move on to approach the throne of God's Grace. However, to enable you to get there, you can either elect to go by sea, via the Faith Boat route, which requires the walking-on-water experience, or you can fly from Faith-Airport, where you get to soar like eagles, under the warm embrace of Yahweh's love, protection, and guidance.

Please note that the 'heavy doubters', or should I say the 'doubterholics', who have overdosed on the things of this world, will be encouraged to go on a strict diet of God's Living Word. I have been reliably informed that the Holy Spirit is on standby to help and support all those who will reach out to His services.

In addition, those travelers who have been found to be without their spiritual passports, testifying to the fact that they are citizens of God's Kingdom, will inevitably experience extra delays. And in fact will have to return to Free Will Train Station, where Jesus will still be patiently waiting for them at 'Christ's Corner'. Once Jesus has gifted them their new spiritual passports/citizenship, their immunization instantly kicks in, and becomes effective against symptoms such as pride, envy, jealousy, unforgiveness, 'hardened heart syndrome', etc.

Everybody will then be cleared to continue with their journey.

That said, please fasten your seatbelts folks, and may I suggest that you read the instruction manual, which is the Holy Bible, before take-off. This will reassure you that any turbulence along the way will not be able to throw you off course or drag you down.

You might be interested to know that the great resistance that you have at your disposal to combat turbulence, (such as sin, worldly mischief, and the pure evil that is inspired and encouraged by the agents of darkness), is again all down to the awesome power of the Holy Spirit.

Also, may I remind you, ladies and gentlemen, of the numerous blessings positioned above your heads. These blessings will automatically drop down when required en-route to both empower and enhance your journey.

Please note that there will be various stops along the way for refuelling, and to replenish. Some of the most popular stops and places of interest you can look forward to are Hope Island, Court of Mercy, Peace Palace, and God's Love Fountain.

Refreshments comprising of the 'Bread of Life' and 'The Pure Water', taken from the 'Springs of Living Water', will also be served.

After this, you will be pleased to learn that you would have arrived at your final destination, where you will be warmly welcomed as you are ushered into Mount Zion, the breathtaking City of the Living God.

Entering the HOLY OF HOLIES, ladies and gentlemen, (and all those who have breath), can you join me in worshipping, adoring, honouring, and praising our Heavenly Father, our Creator, the Living and only True God, and The Great I AM, who is seated on His Majestic Throne.

In addition, 'highly privileged ones', can I categorically say, that this wonderful experience would not have been made possible without the one and only Jesus the Christ, (who is the way, the truth, and the life), and who is seated on the right-hand side of God our Father. So, please People show your appreciation to our Lord and Saviour, who is worthy of the very best of our gratitude and praise for all that he has done for us.

Also in attendance are other distinguished beings, including an innumerable host of Angels, positioned around the throne.

Well, well, ladies and gentlemen, boys and girls, as this is a one-way journey, with no return passage, all that is left for me to say is that it has been an absolute pleasure, and while you experience God's love first hand, please have a wonderful, harmonious, peaceful, joyful, and holy existence, in the presence, and in the sparkling light of God our Father, and our Saviour Jesus Christ.

God bless you all, over and out.

Making Progress

My Father, who reigns above, I throw up praise in prayer

I am so very blessed just by how much you really care

I confess I'm faring well, and my thoughts remain unflawed

This is because I choose to walk daily with you my Lord.

I will refrain from making a fuss, and try to be more mature

I have observed that the more I feast on your word, I need it more
and more

I have not been self-indulgent, nor have I clung on to foolish
pride

I'm just so jubilant that I have Jesus as my Lord and the Holy
Spirit as my guide.

I have refused to engage in squabbles or respond to my worst critic

And even when struck in a vengeful way, I will just turn the other cheek

I have not been awkward or contrary, no sir, that will stay right in the past

I treasure my relationship with my Lord and pray that it will get stronger and will surely last.

I'm bursting with excitement and pleased I'm in a special place

I'm secure, at peace, and comfortable - I feel cherished, loved, and safe

"No weapon fashioned against me shall prosper", it's what I daily declare

And I'm flexing my spiritual muscles, so the enemy had better beware.

I have approached my Father in heaven, and all my progress He has reviewed

But He gently reminded me that there were certain things that I had neglected to include

He said, "child, in addition to your accomplishments, my glorious gospel you'll need to spread

But to achieve the progress that is required, it will mean leaving the comfort of your bed".

Oh!

15. Making Progress

Special Qualifications

Poki Payne had an important meeting and could not afford to be late

For many months, he had been jolly and jobless, and would only procrastinate

In fact, Poki had not only been lazy, but he had flunked all of his major exams

He was also nicknamed 'Phony Poki' because he'd been involved in numerous scams.

But! all was not lost, because, after a few months, Poki had a secret he was keen to share

You see, he'd started going to church, and gave his life to Jesus, during a session of prayer

He then relinquished his cunning ways and was no longer deemed a slob

Instead, a now dapper-looking Poki was to attend an interview for his first legitimate job.

Upon his arrival at the firm, Poki's credentials were immediately examined

So that the interviewer, whose name was Ann, could see if Poki was up for the challenge

Poki confirmed to Ann that in fact, he did have a 'BA' which he had only recently gained

But added that his 'BA brand' was not a bachelor's degree, but it meant he was 'Born Again'.

Bemused, Ann then questioned Poki's claim about him having a master's degree

Poki confessed that his take on this grade strayed from the usual MSc

He revealed to Anne that in his view, it was better than a master of science degree

Because it denoted that Jesus who 'Mastered Sin on the Cross', now rules his destiny.

Intrigued, Ann then questioned Poki about the Ph.D. that he had also declared on his form

Poki replied that he had been empowered by it when others had looked upon him with scorn

He said that his war was no longer with man, but with the unseen enemy who now has to flee

Because his Ph.D. means: 'Power over hosts and demons', and guarantees him victory.

That night as Ann lay restless in her bed, she recalled a certain name

She sensed God had been talking to her all day long, about the man named Poki Payne.

16. Special Qualifications

Bill and Ben,
Two Elderly Gentlemen

Walking in the park, I stumbled upon two elderly men

They were both old-age pensioners, whose names were Bill and Ben

Although I'd never seen them before this very day

Intrigued, I thought I would listen to what they had to say.

Bill was saying, "I can't believe in God because proof I haven't seen

They also say there's heaven and hell, but again I haven't been

Do I believe in miracles? How sure can I really be?

When I really can't trust anyone, except, I, myself, and me."

Ben replied, "they say the sky is blue, but you know I cannot see

They say the grass is green, but how can I agree?

You told me roses are red, but in my mind they're blue

The question is, should I continue to trust myself, or should I rely on you?"

At this point, there is silence, as both men start to eat

And a short while later, in unison, they both rise to their feet

Bill, as usual, takes Ben's hand to lead him on his way

But Ben says, "can you wait a minute, there's something I'd like to say."

'Blind Ben' says "from henceforth I've decided, I will trust my own wit and skill

Because after what we've just discussed, I find I can no longer rely on you Bill"

Bill slightly puzzled says " Ben, the reason that I navigate you is that I'm the one who sees"

Ben responds, "therein lies the problem, because spiritually you're just as blind as me."

17. Bill and Ben, Two Elderly Gentleman

Perfect

Father in heaven,

You are so perfect, and your ways are perfect

Your words are consistently perfect

Our destinies in your hands are perfect

All the plans that you have for us are perfect

The hedges of protection that you pitched around us are perfect

The many blessings you bestow upon us are perfect

Your lovingkindness is pure and perfect

Your thoughts towards us are good and perfect

Your mercies which endure forever are perfect

Your love that engulfs us is so so perfect

It is absolutely right for us to declare that you are author &
perfecter of our faith

And that your gift to us in the form of your precious and perfect
son Jesus Christ

Is mighty,

is amazing

Is glorious,

Is excellent,

Is wonderful,

Is significant,

Is outstanding,

And yes! it is perfect perfection!

Amen

The Heart of Pharaoh

Pharaoh, King of Egypt, was really not amused

Moses, the Lord's servant, had just served him a dose of very bad news

Imagine him stating that the Israelites had to go

With a very hardened heart, Pharaoh simply replied no! no! no!

But, these words came from God, can man then have a say

Oh, believe me, Pharaoh tried, very hard to have his way

And even when smelly blood tainted all his food

It's true, he lost his appetite, but his heart still wasn't moved.

A week later, met Pharaoh, like a lion with a sore head

After he had woken, to find horrors! Frogs had shared his bed

He quickly cried for Moses, who instructed the frogs to depart

But as soon as Pharaoh saw them go, he hardened up his heart.

And then the Lord, through Moses, turned all sand to lice

It was simply everywhere, and folk paid a heavy price

In fact, the Egyptians started moaning, life for them was really rough

Even the magicians couldn't keep up, but still Pharaoh's heart was tough.

Next came a swarm of flies, each like a bumblebee

Clumsily flapping to and fro, and the people couldn't see

The cattle got sick and died, and Pharaoh confessed he was wrong

But when it came to letting the Israelites go, his heart was extra strong.

Then God, via Moses, spread boils, from settled dust and dirt

Pharaoh received a prominent one, right where it really hurt

He tried with God to negotiate another empty deal

But God saw his heart, and it was as hard as ever still.

Rain, hail, fire, and thunder were the next awful plague

And this again put Pharaoh into an awful rage

"The man they call Moses really winds me up," he sighed

"Oh, let them go," he murmured, but then he changed his mind.

Locusts were the next visitors to pop onto the scene

And their job was to eat the crops, oh boy, just weren't they keen

Pharaoh yelled for Moses, "take them away", he groaned

But, when the wind blew them away, his heart was like a stone.

Next came the darkness, when the sun went out of view

The brave men gave out orders, as to what all folk must do

But it was simply no fun, just sleeping for three days

Pharaoh said, "the Israelites can go, but all their cattle stays."

Now during the Passover, the Lord passed the Israelites by

But He struck the first-born sons of the Egyptians, which did cause a huge cry

Pharaoh begged Moses to go and serve, his God who reigns above

And added, "please bless me as you go, for my heart has had enough."

18. The Heart of Pharaoh

God Knows Best

Some brethren want to preach and teach

And do everything themselves

Some brethren may not accept God's will

And look for something else

But what we want may not be the best

And it is certainly not the key

If we really, truly want to be

What we were born to be.

Some brethren think they're professionals

And go the Christian walk alone

Even though they may plan the greatest crusade

Without God, they're on their own

And even with all the benefits of their crusade

It's still not worth leaving their lane

Because every time we divert from God's plan

Our work may be in vain.

Our primary assignment is to be

A living sacrifice

Holy acceptable unto God

On offer is our life

We might not be crusaders now

Though this may later be God's will

Just be willing to be used by God

Basically, that's the deal.

It's our secondary assignment

That God tells us what to do

He can also send us

To certain places too

But wherever we're sent, we must return

Once we know we really ought

Because as a servant our work is varied

And after each job, we must report.

Though you may feel you are busy

Stop and respond to God's call

Because with all your best intentions

Without God, you're bound to fall

The Israelites were in the wilderness

For an awfully long time

And they only entered the promised land

When they decided to toe God's line.

Again, stepping back in History

We meet men like Abraham

Who learnt all about this lesson

So was always in God's plan

There is much more work for us to do today

So, stay in your lane with care

So that when God comes looking just for you

You will always be right there.

My Schedule
For Today

It's time to awake and investigate what I've got planned today

So, I'm going downstairs to consult my schedule without any further delay

As I feed on the word, my spirit-man, will stay strong and be blessed

But I will clamp down heavily, and will not give an inch, but crucify my flesh.

Poor attitudes I will toss aside and publicly I will disown

But I will try and be more Christ-like and follow Christ alone

To my enemies, I will apologize and also make amends

And in this process, I will turn them into my beloved and dearest friends.

I will kick it to the kerb, and in addition, will also reject all pride

But I will run to 'humility', knock on its door, and in it, I will hide

I will turn my back on the whole wide world, that will be my personal choice

But I will pay attention to the Holy Spirit, and obey His still small voice.

I will stand my ground and also offer up no apology

For resisting the enemy and his underhand tactics and watch him simply flee

I am not speaking figuratively when I declare that my temper I will lose

But I plan to find that virtue of 'endurance', so when ticked-off, that's what I use.

I will be ruthless with 'selfishness', and will promptly show it the door

But I will cling onto 'generosity' and help the needy and the poor

I will not entertain, or connive with the wild thoughts going round in my head

They will definitely get no 'head-time' but will receive their marching orders instead.

These are the items that I have listed, on my schedule, for today

but to get to the dizzy heights of success, I must fall on my knees and pray.

Jesus!
Born in Bethlehem

Christmas is here again

Snowflakes falling now and then

Folks are rushing, rushing here and there

Such a hectic scene

Is this the Christmas theme?

Or the fact that Jesus was born in Bethlehem.

At Christmas, greetings we share

To show just how much we care

Is this the real Christmas, or Christmassy theme?

Cos, recall that special morn

When Jesus Christ was born

Angels spread tidings about Christ's birth in Bethlehem.

At Christmas, gifts are bought

With loving care and thought

For our loved ones, friends, and families

Similarly, some wise men came from far

Following a star

With gifts for Jesus, born in Bethlehem.

Food and parties are the trends

In attendance are the Ladies and Gentlemen

Is this why we have Christmas, or is this the Christmas theme?

What a massive party scene

In Heaven, there must have been

When our King Jesus was born in Bethlehem.

You see, Jesus came down to save man

It was his Father's perfect plan

Hallelujah Jesus was born in Bethlehem.

And yes, He later died for me

Broke those chains and set me free

Thank God that Jesus was born in Bethlehem.

Join me in praising Jesus

Happy Birthday Jesus

Hallelujah, Jesus was born in Bethlehem.

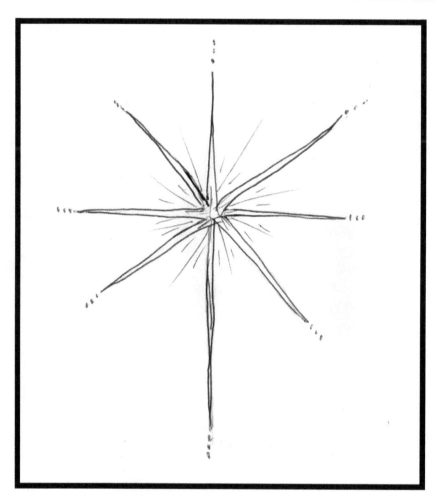

19. Jesus! born in Bethlehem

My Good Deeds

Praise the Lord, It's a brand-new year

My main priority is to care, care, care

For my family, friends, and folks I don't know

It can be at home, at work, wherever I go.

So, it's Monday evening and I'm home at last

It was grueling at work, but I've done my day's task

But there's a knock on the door, I opened to find my neighbour
Sam

After a cupper, he told me he was in a bit of a jam.

His main problem was money or the lack of it

He was in arrears with his rent because his job he just quit

I offered to pray, and reassured him that things will improve

But Sam looked quite doubtful as he was told he must move.

I suppose I could have helped Sam in a more practical way

But I won't ponder on that, It's another new day

So, when my friend Sue told me, she was in a very tight spot

I promised to support her in prayer, but then completely forgot.

Wednesday: Yet for Jesus, no soul have I gained

Could I possibly share the gospel right here on this train?

I decided against it, as my day had been tough

But then, this chap shared with me some extreme radical stuff.

Thursday: And now there's this guy on the street

Who, to my trained eye, looked drunk and was quite unsteady on his feet

Should I go over and tell him that Jesus can surely set him free?

But, as his eyes rolled around, I thought it better just to flee.

Friday: I'm in a cafe with 'single mum' Meg

Who immediately seemed interested in the scriptures I'd read

But our time was cut short cos her toddler became peeved

After throwing his food at the waiter, it was suggested we leave.

Saturday: The week has gone, and I reluctantly confess

That it fell short of being classed as a roaring success

But hey, I've just been in prayer, and God's face did I seek

Guess what? He said, "with my help, you'll move mountains next week."

20. My Good Deeds

Let's be careful
with the things God gives us

Roy, Roy, a noble gent

Packed his load and off he went

To a distant place, to receive some land

He was to have, all was planned.

But Roy, Roy, before he did go

Called his servants and told them so

That they should all receive a pound

And occupy all of his ground.

Roy, Roy, the land he got

He then returned home to his own lot

He called his servants, the ones he paid

To see the profits they have made.

"Paul, Paul, I'm back what's new

The pound I gave, how did you do?"

"Master, I worked night and day

I've got ten pounds, I'm glad to say."

"Well done, my faithful man

For you, I have a tremendous plan"

The second servant had this to say

"I've gained five pounds, is that okay?"

"Yes, yes," Roy confessed

"So far I am well impressed"

But then came his servant Guy

Who had a glint in his eye.

"Sir, sir, that's not the way to go

To reap what you did not sow"

Without delay, with his face all set

He produced the pound which he had kept.

"Guy, Guy, I'm unfair, you say?

Then why not put the money away?

In a savings place or a bank, I guess

And then I could have had interest."

"Staff, staff, hear what I say

Guy here's thrown a good chance away"

Give his pound to my servant Paul

And Guy will end up with nothing at all."

Luke 19:12-26

Court

Tomorrow I start my trial, I wonder how I'll cope

I'm shaky, afraid, and nervous, I've been told that I don't have "a hope"

I don't even have a case, and bail was immediately denied

I was told that the preponderance of the evidence supported the other side.

My solicitor just briefed me that I should expect the very worst

He was even less encouraging when I revealed my empty purse

Here I am filled with sadness, separated and alone

I'm in prison, broke and in debt, they've taken everything I own.

Oh God, I have tried to resolve my issues, and from jail, this is a desperate cry

My God replied, "perhaps, my dear, you might fancy giving me a try"

"But Lord, is it not too late? Is my future not too bleak?"

My Heavenly Father said, "trust me, my child, and lie down and go to sleep."

As I succumbed to sleep, I had this wonderful dream

Whereby I was in the dock with this terrific legal team

Where Jesus was the advocate, and the Angels were the jury

The Judge was our Heavenly Father, surrounded by all His glory.

Then there's silence! as the Judge spoke from His Magnificent Throne

He quietly said, "child, we've been expecting you, you're not here on your own

This is not a Law Court, this is a Court of Grace

No harm will overcome you because I will keep you safe."

He then set His gaze on me, and asked: "how do you plead?"

I remembered my – hmm – colourful past, and pleaded guilty as can be

"There are loads of dodgy things I've done Lord, but the worst offense in my view

Is stubbornly struggling on my Lord, separating myself from you."

"Well my child, Jesus, My Son, has pleaded your very case

Not only that, He's done your time, just believe and keep your faith

The laws of the land you may still have to face, this Court has set you free

Now wake up child, you're not alone, because we are now your family."

21.. Court

Eternal
Salvation

In His own image, God created man

And with good thoughts towards him, commenced a plan

Adam was God's first human creation

And thus, begins our journey to our Eternal Salvation.

After Adam, God our Father created Eve

So that she could be Adam's helpmate, and from his side never leave

And to create Eve, God undertook his first medical operation

Which will continue Man's journey to Eternal Salvation.

By being deceived by Satan, Eve landed in real trouble

As her actions then burst God's protective bubble

Which led further to the big separation

But, undeterred, God continued His plans for our Eternal Salvation.

But God tackling the challenges of man's life-changing sin

Was not fazed, but threw a new destiny for man in the ring

Displaying unwavering but focused dedication

Which then catapulted us closer to our Eternal Salvation.

But the devil is an accuser, to both you and to me

He showed his utter contempt for God's love, which we could all clearly see

He put forward his own cynical objection

Nevertheless, his actions aided Man's quest for Eternal Salvation.

You see, the devil could not grasp the concept, against God he could not win

And he had no idea that Jesus had agreed to die for our sin

However, to accomplish this, Jesus had to undergo a public crucifixion

which further led to Man's claim to Eternal Salvation.

And so, folks, this narrative does not abruptly end here

Because on Easter Sunday, the stone that guarded the burial ground of Jesus was rolled away clear

And Jesus arose from the dead, which the scriptures refer to as His resurrection

Which directly leads us all to our Eternal Salvation.

22. Eternal Salvation

Followers of Christ

If a flurry of thoughts try to gate-crash your mind

Cast them out if they're thoughts you don't wish Jesus to find

If you jump on your soapbox and shout out real loud

Make sure whatever you're saying will make Jesus proud.

Those books that you read, please make perfectly sure

That they will not defile you, but instead help keep your thoughts pure

If you're invited to a gathering, even if it's just 'bring and share'

Still, politely decline if Jesus does not want you there.

Whatever your hobbies, be they plenty or few

Please shut them right down if you have some explaining to do

Also, think about those days when you're seriously bored

Try to resist doing those things, which will displease our Lord.

If you've been praying about something, albeit you've been praying amiss

Don't waste God's time or yours, but scrub it off your prayer list

When you've reached a place where flesh and spirit's in dispute

Make sure you don't end up heading down the wrong path or wrong route.

In life, don't present as a victim, or believe you've been framed

Just because God caught you doing something, for which you are now deeply ashamed

Brethren, when our Lord returns, will your words to him be

I've been able to live for you Lord, only because you first died for me.

23. Followers of Christ

Thank You

Dear Lord, did I thank you for the blessings you constantly provide?

See how all species look to you alone, to live and to survive

The trees that are known specifically by their unique, but various fruits

And the flowers adorned in their brightly coloured dresses and smart designer suits.

Lord, did I thank you for the animals that we see all around?

Either in the sea, or in the sky, or with us right here on the ground

It is common knowledge that animals can be a threat when they then become new mums

But they turn into the biggest softies and are very tender towards their young.

Although birds can sing acapella style, they can still keep their sweet notes

The toads join in, with the occasional, but very distinguished croaks

And what about the rainbow that tends to drop by, immediately after the rains

And those delicate snowflakes, that slow dance across acres & acres of plains.

Dear Lord, did I actually thank you for the sun that shines so bright?

And when the day turns in, the moon steps out, producing a string of dainty light

How amazing are the numerous stars that tend to twinkle now and then?

And when their twinkling is all but done, the sun steps out again.

Dear Lord, I really want to thank you for all that you have done

To save my soul, you did not withhold your only begotten son

So, thank you Lord for opening my eyes and then letting me see

The beauty of your creation, and the extreme love you have for me.